4.2   2001 $16.80

THE
HUNT *for* FOOD

ANITA GANERI
ILLUSTRATED BY GRAHAM AUSTIN

The Millbrook Press
Brookfield, Connecticut

Published in the United States in 1997 by

The Millbrook Press, Inc.
2 Old New Milford Road
Brookfield, Connecticut 06804

First published in Great Britain in 1994 by

Belitha Press Limited
London House
Great Eastern Wharf
Parkgate Road
London SW11 4NQ

Editor: Rachel Cooke
Designer: Frances McKay
Consultant: Steve Pollock

Library of Congress Cataloging-in-Publication Data

Ganeri, Anita, 1961–
      The hunt for food / Anita Ganeri ; illustrated by Graham Austin.
         p.   cm. — (Life's cycles)
      Includes index.
      Summary: Describes the interdependence among plants and animals
living in a meadow environment, from spring to winter.
         ISBN 0-7613-0304-9 (lib. bdg.)
      1. Food chains (Ecology)—Juvenile literature.   2. Meadow ecology—
Juvenile literature.   [1. Food chains (Ecology)   2. Meadow
ecology.   3. Ecology.]   I. Austin, Graham, ill.   II. Title.
III. Series.
QH541.14.G36   1997
577.4'616—dc21
                                                                            97-13058
                                                                               CIP
                                                                                AC

CONTENTS

EATING FOR ENERGY

All animals have to eat. They need food to stay alive. Food gives them energy and helps them to grow and to stay healthy. Many animals spend a great deal of time looking for food—and avoiding being eaten themselves.

The way animals are linked together by what they eat is called a **food chain.** But at the start of every food chain are plants. Unlike animals, plants can make their own food, using energy from the Sun, in a process called **photosynthesis**. **Chlorophyll**, a green substance which gives plants their color, captures sunlight and uses it with water and **carbon dioxide** gas from the air to make the food that plants need to live.

The energy stored by the plants as food is passed on to the animal that eats them and, in turn, to whatever animal eats it. So energy is passed along the food chain. A very simple food chain is shown here.

The fox gets energy by eating the mouse.

The Sun gives plants the energy they need to make their food.

Words in **bold** are explained in the glossary on pages 28-29.

The mouse gets energy by eating the plants.

Plants make their food using the Sun's energy, water, and carbon dioxide from the air.

Most animals have a mixed **diet**. So they link into lots of different food chains. These interlinking chains form what is called a **food web**. Food chains and food webs are an important part of the natural world. Each one is different depending on the surroundings or **environment** it is in. This could be a meadow, a forest, or the ocean. Through the pages of this book, you can discover the food web that is created in one of these environments, the meadow.

A SIMPLE FOOD WEB

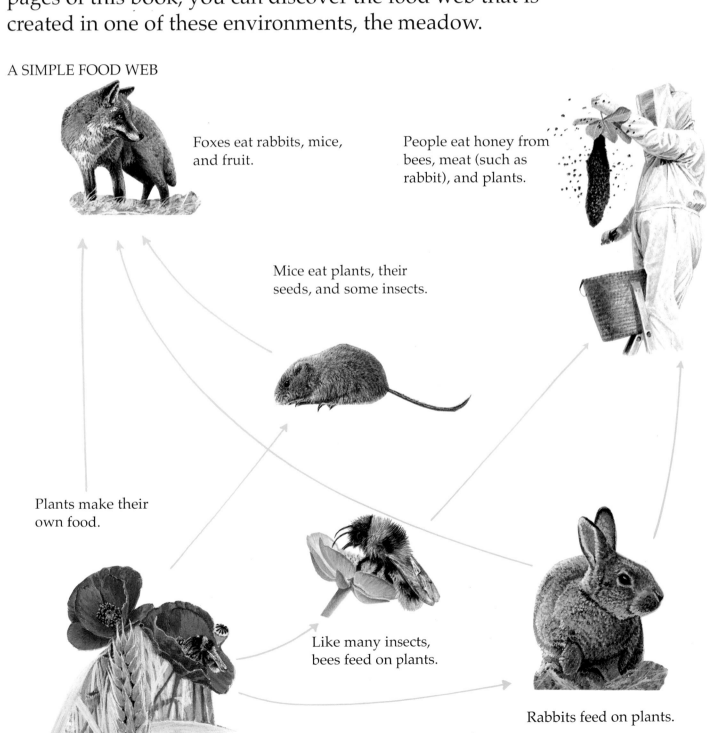

Foxes eat rabbits, mice, and fruit.

People eat honey from bees, meat (such as rabbit), and plants.

Mice eat plants, their seeds, and some insects.

Plants make their own food.

Like many insects, bees feed on plants.

Rabbits feed on plants.

THE MEADOW

Welcome to the meadow. With its lush grass, hedges, and flowers, it attracts a large variety of animals looking for food. Apart from the grazing cows, how many animals and plants can you find in the picture? You'll see them many times throughout the book as we follow their lives. Read the story and connect the pictures on different pages and you'll discover the food web of the meadow.

Here, the meadow is shown in high summer, but it changes constantly. Through the year, as each season passes, the meadow plants grow and flower, while the feeding animals come and go.

NEW GROWTH

The story begins early in the year. Winter is coming to an end in the meadow. The weather is still cold and frosty. But the meadow is not as lifeless as it seems. Some plants are starting to grow. Seeds and bulbs put out roots and shoots. The grass is growing again. And a bird is busily **gorging** itself on yellow catkins —a sure sign that spring is coming.

A welcome shower of rain has provided the plants with water which they need to grow. The Sun is shining through the clouds. The growing plants need the energy in sunlight to make their food.

This acorn is putting out its first root. If it survives, it will grow into a huge oak tree. The seed uses food stored inside it to grow until it sprouts some leaves. Then it can begin to make its own food. ▼

This finch is out looking for food. It uses its tweezer-like beak to peck up seeds or, in this case, snip off and eat the hazel catkins.

◄ Snowdrops and daffodils grow from bulbs. These are chunky stems which remain underground during the winter, alive but not growing. They contain stores of food to give the plant the energy to grow again.

▼ The hazel tree twigs are covered in bright yellow catkins. These are male flowers, full of pollen. The wind shakes the pollen from the catkins and carries it away. If the pollen lands on a female flower, a seed can develop—the hazel nut. This might grow into a new hazel tree, but it could also make a meal for a hungry animal.

This ground beetle grub hunts ▶ for food underground. It lives off slugs, roots, and other grubs. It feeds and grows for several months until it is time to turn into an adult.

The edible snail has many enemies, including foxes, birds, and people. It spends the winter in a snug underground burrow, sealed in its shell by a door of **mucus**.

FEEDING BEGINS

Now the meadow is waking up. As the warmer spring weather arrives, animals become more active. The search for food has begun. They are hungry after the long winter when there was very little to eat. There is plenty of food now that the plants are growing again. But the animals need to stay alert. Further up the food chain, other animals called **predators** such as foxes are hungry, too.

▼ The harvest mouse has left its winter nest to look for seeds and bulbs to eat. It hides behind the plant stems.

▲ Moles spend most of their lives tunnelling underground. As they dig, they sniff and feel out earthworms to eat.

◀ This squirrel has uncovered the acorn that was putting down its first root. The acorn won't grow into an oak tree, but it will give the squirrel energy.

◀ The rabbit munches away on fresh young plant leaves and grass. It needs plenty of energy as it will soon give birth to its young. As it eats, it keeps a constant lookout for danger.

▼ Molehills are a common sight in the meadow. They are small humps of soil which the mole pushes to the surface, out of the way. The mole often pushes up extra large hills above its food store.

▼ The mole stores any spare earthworms it catches in a special burrow. It bites off their heads to keep them from wriggling away. A mole can eat its weight in worms in a day.

▲ Earthworms eat their way through the soil. They **digest** any useful bits and push the rest out of their bodies. This keeps the soil healthy so more plants can grow.

GREEN LEAVES

Spring is in the air. Everywhere you look there's something growing. Animals are beginning to give birth to their young. More of the plants and trees are putting out leaves. The meadow is filled with the chirping song of birds looking for a mate. Some birds have only just returned to the meadow after spending the winter somewhere warmer.

◄ The swallows begin to arrive. They are spring and summer visitors to the meadow. They have spent the winter in a warmer part of the world, where they could find insects to eat. Now they will be able to catch plenty of insects here.

▼ A fox has entered the meadow. It has followed its nose to the rabbit's burrow. Foxes have a superb sense of smell. They use it to hunt both by day and by night.

▼ The rabbit hides in its underground burrow, waiting for the fox to go away. It would not stand a chance in the fox's sharp teeth.

◄ Baby rabbits are born underground, safe from attack. They stay in their nursery burrow until they are old enough to fend for themselves.

◄ The hazel's leaves have come out in the warm spring weather.

▲ Leaves contain the green chlorophyll that plants need to make food. The plant holds out its leaves so that the maximum sunlight possible falls upon them. The chlorophyll captures the energy in the sunlight and uses it to make food with water from the soil and carbon dioxide from the air.

▼ A thrush uses its strong beak to pull out a worm.

◄ The hazel's roots spread out deep into the ground. The roots **extract** water and **minerals** from the soil. The plant needs these to grow. The water passes up the roots and through the stem to the leaves, where it can be used for photosynthesis.

FOOD FOR THE YOUNG

The meadow is a lively place as spring turns into summer. The female thrush lays eggs in her new nest. Then she keeps them warm until they hatch. The young birds are always hungry. They keep their parents very busy. Butterflies, bees, and grasshoppers all feed in the meadow now. There's danger, too. The fox is determined to catch a rabbit!

◄ ▲ While the female bird sits on her eggs, the male chirps and calls. This warns other animals to stay away from the nest and not to harm the eggs.

▼ Grasshoppers feed on plant leaves. They use their long legs to jump away from enemies to avoid being eaten themselves.

► The female butterfly lays her eggs on nettle leaves. Stinging hairs on the leaves keep most animals from eating the leaves—and the eggs.

◄ The chase is on! The rabbit will soon be the hungry fox's next meal. Foxes also eat squirrels, insects, and eggs.

▼ Now the eggs are hatched, and the parent birds bring food to their hungry babies. Meals include worms and caterpillars.

A bee lands on a bramble blossom. Its long tongue sucks up syrupy **nectar** from deep inside the flower. The nectar produced by the meadow's flowers attracts many insects. In return for the food, the insects help the flowers to produce their seeds. ▼

▲ Juicy snails are the adult thrush's favorite food. They smash the shells open on large stones. The birds use the same stones again and again. The ground nearby is littered with broken shells.

◄ The newly-hatched caterpillars eat their eggshells first. Then they munch their way through the nettle leaves. They spend all their time feeding. But not all the caterpillars will live to be butterflies. Too many birds, such as the thrush, like to eat them.

FULL BLOOM

It is high summer and the meadow is in full bloom. The cows are grazing on the lush, green grass. They provide people with milk to drink. A harvest mouse is building its summer nest among the corn stalks. The caterpillars have stopped eating. It's time for them to spin their **cocoons.** But the young birds are still hungry!

▼ A boy enjoys a summer picnic—a glass of milk and a cheese sandwich. The cheese is made from milk. Cows provide us with lots of different food to eat.

◀ The harvest mouse builds its ball-shaped nest out of corn stalks. It shreds these with its teeth.

▼ The caterpillar will soon spin its cocoon. Inside, it will not eat but use its stored up energy to change into an adult butterfly.

▼ The ground beetle has changed from a grub into an adult beetle. It hunts for slugs and small insects.

◀ There is plenty of food now for the snail. It crawls up and down the plant stems, eating as it goes.

► The young thrush has grown most of its feathers, but its wings and tail are too short for it to fly very far. Food is still provided by its parents.

▼ The farmer keeps the grassy meadow for his cows. There are nearly always some there, chewing the **cud.** Grass is tough to digest so cows have several large stomachs to grind it up. Grass gives cows the energy to produce milk.

▼ The cow pats in the meadow are also useful. Flies use cow pats as warm, safe places to lay their eggs. They are also a rich source of food when the **maggots** hatch.

▼ The rabbits are enjoying a feast. For once there is no danger from the fox. They chew grass, which is their main food, with their flat back teeth.

DANGER ABOVE

A new animal has entered the world of the meadow. High in the sky, a falcon hovers. Its sharp eyes search the field for the small animals it likes to eat. Has it seen the plump young birds, or the harvest mouse? This tiny creature has left its nest to feed on the ripening corn growing wild at the edge of the meadow.

◄ As the bee feeds on nectar, the flower's pollen sticks to stiff hairs on the bee's back legs. The bee can now take pollen to other flowers it visits, allowing these flowers to produce seeds. The bee does the same job as the wind did for the hazel.

▲ The falcon is a fierce hunter. It uses its superb eyesight to look for rodents, birds, and insects to eat. Its sharp, hooked beak is ideal for tearing meat.

► The young thrush has all its adult feathers. It can fly now, but not very far. It is also beginning to hunt for its own food, but it still relies partly on its parents.

▲ After two to three weeks, the **chrysalis** splits open. An adult butterfly crawls out. Soon it will feed on the nectar it finds in the meadow's flowers.

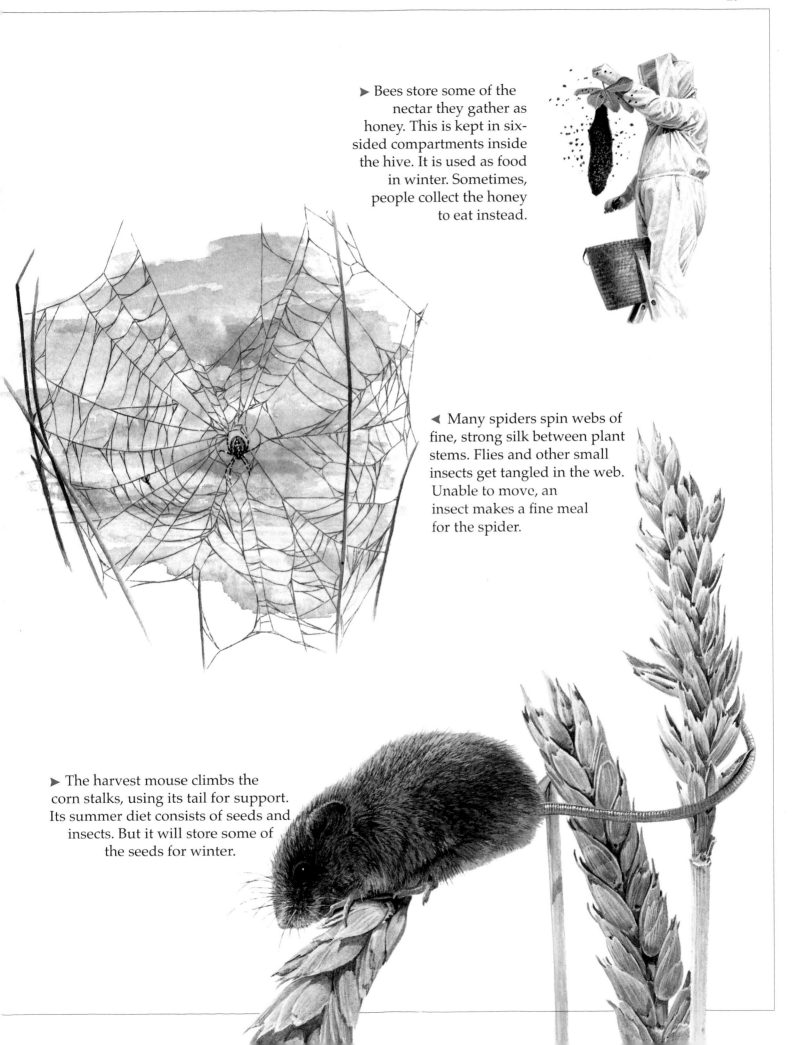

► Bees store some of the
nectar they gather as
honey. This is kept in six-
sided compartments inside
the hive. It is used as food
in winter. Sometimes,
people collect the honey
to eat instead.

◄ Many spiders spin webs of
fine, strong silk between plant
stems. Flies and other small
insects get tangled in the web.
Unable to move, an
insect makes a fine meal
for the spider.

► The harvest mouse climbs the
corn stalks, using its tail for support.
Its summer diet consists of seeds and
insects. But it will store some of
the seeds for winter.

FRUIT FOR EVERYONE

The weather has turned cooler and the days are getting shorter. Autumn is on its way. This is the time when the meadow plants produce their fruit and seeds. Some seeds will survive the winter and grow into new plants next spring. But a great many will be eaten by the meadow animals or stored away for the winter.

▼ The blackberries on the bramble bush contain seeds. Many animals eat the berries and pass the seeds out through their bodies. Some will grow into new brambles. Blackberries are very tasty in pies.

▼ A ladybug's color warns birds that it is nasty to eat.

▼ The poppy flowers have died and the seedheads have formed. They look like pepper shakers. The seeds are shaken out and scattered by the wind.

▲ The hazel tree's flowers grow
into nuts. Squirrels gnaw holes
in the shells to reach the
juicy part inside. Other
animals feed on the
nuts, too. The
nuthatch is
one example.

▲ Fungi, such as
toadstools and mushrooms, grow in the
meadow. Fungi feed off dead plant and
animal matter. This helps the process of
rot, which returns the goodness in the
matter to the soil.

◄ A grasshopper's color
camouflages it on a grass stem,
and hides it from hungry enemies.

▲ The fox has turned its attention away from the rabbit
for a minute. It is feasting on blackberries instead. Foxes
are not just meat eaters. They can't always catch enough
to survive, so they eat plants as well.

GATHERING FOR WINTER

As the autumn days pass, the trees in the meadow begin to change color. Their leaves do not make food in the cold winter, so they die and fall off. A rabbit falls **prey** to the patient fox and the sharp-eyed falcon is in the perfect place to swoop down on the harvest mouse. Slowly the meadow prepares for the cold winter months ahead.

◄ As food becomes scarcer, swallows collect in huge flocks ready to fly away to warmer places. They return to the meadow in spring.

▼ The fox catches and kills another rabbit. This may be the fox's only meal for some time, so it makes the most of it.

► The squirrel continues to feed on nuts. It stores some as well, hiding them away to eat later in the winter.

▼ The changing seasons do not affect the mole much. It stays underground, hunting for worms. From time to time, it comes up to rummage among the fallen leaves.

▲ The ground is covered with fallen leaves. The ground beetle feeds on some, but most rot. This helps to make the soil rich and dark for the next crop of meadow plants.

◄ In autumn, the leaves change color from green to shades of red and russet and gold. Then they die. Freezing temperatures prevent them from making food.

▲ Hovering high above the ground, the falcon sees a young harvest mouse far below. Any minute now the falcon will swoop down and pounce.

▼ Some mushrooms are good to eat (although others are **poisonous,** so don't risk trying any). The young harvest mouse is so busy nibbling a mushroom it does not notice the danger overhead.

◄ One rabbit is safe underground, out of sight of the fox. It is warm and snug out of the autumn chill.

SURVIVING THE COLD

Finally, winter comes to the meadow. It is very cold and there is very little for the animals to eat. Some creatures survive the winter by **hibernating.** Other animals don't actually hibernate but they do sleep for days on end. This saves energy and their stores of food. It is very quiet as the meadow and its **inhabitants** wait for spring to come again.

▶ A **solitary** thrush sings in the bare branches of the hazel. Its abandoned nest is easy to find now that there are no leaves to hide it.

◀ A large flock of lapwings flies over the meadow. They will feed here and on the surrounding plowed fields in winter. Lapwings are also known as peewits, because of the sound they make.

▼ This mouse has not survived the winter. As its body decays, it puts goodness into the soil, making it richer. Nothing is wasted in the meadow. Perhaps some of the poppy seeds shaken from their seedheads will sprout here in the spring.

▼ Another harvest mouse is collecting food for its winter store. These animals do not hibernate, but they spend most of the winter in their underground burrows.

◄ The winter cold would kill the butterflies, so they hibernate from October to March. They find a crack in a hollow tree and stay there until the spring sunshine wakes them up.

▲ There's the chance of a rare feast for the fox. It usually has a hard job finding enough food to eat in winter. But it may catch the squirrel off guard.

▲ The leaves die and fall off the trees, leaving the branches bare and brown. The trees conserve their energy through the winter, ready to burst into bud again when the warm weather comes.

► The squirrel spends most of the winter asleep in its nest. It only comes out to look for nuts it has hidden (if it can remember where) or any left lying on the ground.

THE FOOD WEB

A whole year has passed and the meadow and its food web have come full circle through four seasons. The cycle begins again in spring. Here you can see the whole of the meadow's **complex** food web. Lots of energy has been passed among the plants and animals during the year. This is a process that never stops—it is one of life's cycles.

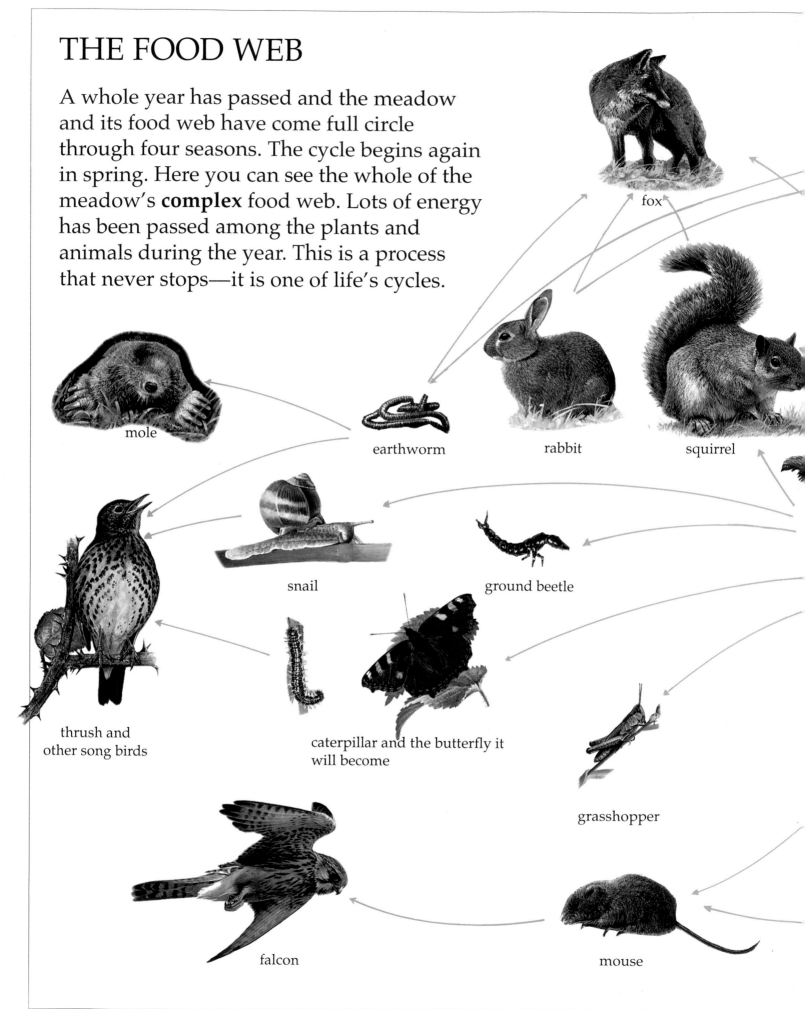

fox

mole

earthworm

rabbit

squirrel

snail

ground beetle

thrush and
other song birds

caterpillar and the butterfly it
will become

grasshopper

falcon

mouse

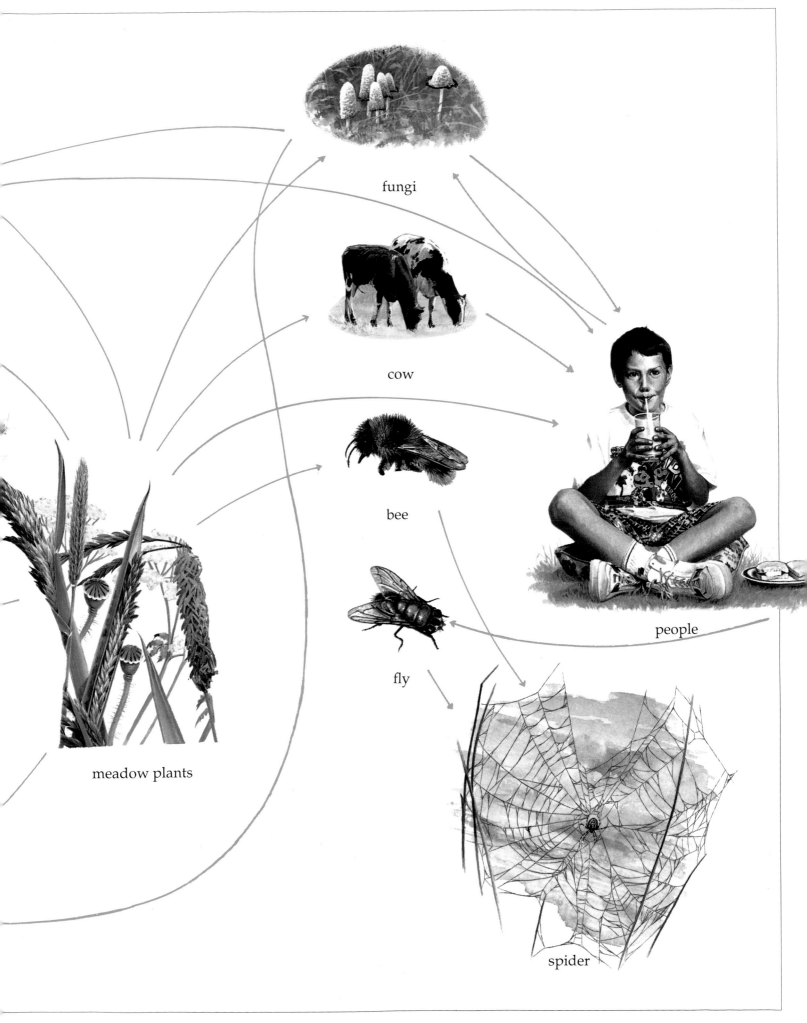

fungi

cow

bee

fly

people

meadow plants

spider

GLOSSARY

camouflage Being the same color as your surroundings so that you can hide from predators.

carbon dioxide One of the gases in the air. It is used by plants during **photosynthesis**. Animals release carbon dioxide into the air when they breathe out.

chlorophyll The green substance in plants. Chlorophyll traps the energy in sunlight and uses it to turn water and carbon dioxide into sugar and oxygen. This process is called **photosynthesis**.

chrysalis The stage in the growth of a moth or butterfly between when it is a caterpillar and when it is fully grown. The caterpillar fixes itself to a stem and forms a **cocoon** around itself. While it is inside, the chrysalis changes into a butterfly or moth.

cocoon The protective case that a caterpillar spins around itself. Inside the cocoon the caterpillar becomes a **chrysalis** and then turns into a butterfly or moth.

complex Made up of many parts.

cud Grass which has been chewed by a cow, stored in its first stomach, and then chewed again.

diet The food and drink that a creature needs to live.

digest To break down food so that animals can use it for growth and energy.

environment The surroundings or place in which animals live.

extract To take out of.

food chain A series of living things that depend on each other for food. A rabbit eats grass and a fox eats rabbits. This is a food chain.

food web A number of food chains that are linked. A living thing may eat many different living things and may be eaten by lots of other living things. A bird may eat berries, plants, insects, or fish. The bird may then be eaten by foxes, cats, or people. These food chains make up a food web.

gorging Eating food quickly and greedily.

hibernate To spend the winter asleep.

inhabitants The animals or people that live in a place.

maggots The soft, thick, worm-like bodies of larvae. A larva is a grub which grows into a fly.

minerals Natural substances found in the ground that do not come from animals or plants. Iron and salt are minerals.

mucus A clear, slimy liquid produced by some creatures to protect themselves.

nectar A sugary liquid produced by flowers. Bees and other insects collect nectar to make honey (for food).

photosynthesis The process by which plants make food, using the **chlorophyll** in their leaves, sunlight, carbon dioxide, and water.

poisonous Something which causes harm to living things when they eat or touch it.

predator An animal that hunts other animals for food.

prey Animals which are hunted and eaten for food by other animals.

solitary Alone; not in a group.

INDEX

Words in **bold** appear
in the glossary on
pages 28 and 29